# IDIOMS DELIGHT

## JOHN ARENA

This book was conceived and begun by John Arena before his untimely death. It has been my privilege and pleasure to put on the finishing touches.

Betty Lou Kratoville
Senior Editor

**Cover and interior illustrations: Steven Mundy**

High Noon Books
A Division of Academic Therapy Publications
20 Commercial Blvd.
Novato, CA 94949

International Standard Book Number: 0-87879-889-7

11 10 09 08 07 06 05
20 19 18 17 16 15 14 13

# Introduction

Idioms have become so much a part of our English language that most of us are probably unaware of how frequently we use them. Phrases such as "bury the hatchet," "play second fiddle," "out on a limb" slide into social and business conversations easily and unnoticed, bringing color and flavor to the language—and brevity, too. (How much quicker to say, "I draw a blank" than "I don't understand what they are talking about.") However, idioms are appropriate and useful only when they are understood equally well by both the speaker and the listener (or the writer and the reader).

Several types of students may be unfamiliar or may experience difficulty with idioms: (1) youngsters with learning disabilities, who are notably literal; (2) children from backgrounds in which English is the second language; (3) students whose inadequate social skills stem at least in part from limited language development. Although all of these youngsters may be exposed to idioms in television programs, in films, and in everyday encounters, whether or not they *understand* what they hear is debatable.

Idioms are colorful and fun and can be a lighthearted part of the daily curriculum. The seventy-five idioms (in six lessons) presented in this book were selected from literally hundreds to be found in the English language, and the student is encouraged in all six lessons to add to the list. By the time the class has completed all of the activities in the book, students may have compiled a list of several hundred additional idioms and be able to compile a book of their own!

Idioms are not always easy to define. Sometimes there are subtleties that defy a precise definition. Consequently, the teacher would be well advised to schedule ample discussion time for each lesson before the written exercises are attempted so that students feel at ease with idioms they are about to use, possibly for the first time.

A number of supplementary activities can be included. For example, let students take turns reading idioms aloud to decide which ones are spoken in anger; which ones in a whisper; which ones with resignation; which ones despondently—or cheerfully. At the completion of the six lessons, one field-tested class wrote an entire one-act play and somehow managed to use all seventy-five idioms presented in *Idiom's Delight*. Idioms can be great fun to illustrate (try "He throws his weight around") and lend themselves to simple doggerel or rhyme. (Many a substitute teacher has been pleased to find *Idiom's Delight* as part of the lesson plans that were left for her, and many a regular classroom teacher has found the book a blessing in the trying days just before a holiday.)

No special instructions are needed for the exercises, all of which are self-explanatory. (Each set of six lessons is followed by its own answer key for the teacher's convenience.) The only particular direction the teacher is urged to follow is that of "tone." It would be regrettable if a lesson on idioms turned out to be ponderous and heavy, for the material was designed to lend itself generally to good humor and cheer. The title, *Idiom's Delight,* is a harbinger, it is hoped, of things to come.

## What Idioms Mean

I'm cooling my heels.

| | | |
|---|---|---|
| **Keep your shirt on** | *means* | Wait a minute; stay calm |
| **Go fly a kite** | *means* | Get away from me; leave me alone |
| **Can't cut the mustard** | *means* | Can't measure up to expectations; can't do it |
| **My hands are tied** | *means* | I can't do anything about it |
| **Time on my hands** | *means* | I've plenty of time; I've nothing special to do |
| **You're pulling my leg** | *means* | You're joking |
| **Step on it!** | *means* | Hurry! |
| **Hold your horses** | *means* | Wait a minute |
| **Too many irons in the fire** | *means* | Trying to do too many things all at one time |
| **In a jam** | *means* | In trouble |
| **Let your hair down** | *means* | Relax and share your thoughts and problems |
| **Lost his marbles** | *means* | Acts as if he's crazy |
| **Eat your words** | *means* | You said something and now you wish you hadn't said it |
| **Face the music** | *means* | Be brave; take what's coming |
| **Cool your heels** | *means* | Wait |

Name _____ Date_____

# Matching

*Draw a line to connect the idiom to its correct meaning. The first one has been done for you.*

## A

| | |
|---|---|
| Cool your heels | Relax and share your thoughts and problems |
| Eat your words | In trouble |
| Let your hair down | Wait a minute; stay calm |
| In a jam | Wait |
| Keep your shirt on | You said something and now you wish you hadn't said it |

## B

| | |
|---|---|
| Face the music | Wait a minute |
| Lost his marbles | Hurry! |
| Hold your horses | Be brave; take what's coming |
| Step on it! | I've plenty of time; I've nothing to do |
| Time on my hands | Acts as if he is crazy |

## C

| | |
|---|---|
| Go fly a kite | Can't measure up to expectations; can't do it |
| Can't cut the mustard | You're joking |
| My hands are tied | I can't do anything about it |
| You're pulling my leg | Trying to do too many things at one time |
| Too many irons in the fire | Get away from me; leave me alone |

Name _____ Date_____

# Which One Fits?

| | | |
|---|---|---|
| **Keep your shirt on** | *means* | Wait a minute; stay calm |
| **Go fly a kite** | *means* | Get away from me; leave me alone |
| **Can't cut the mustard** | *means* | Can't measure up to expectations; can't do it |
| **My hands are tied** | *means* | I can't do anything about it |
| **Time on my hands** | *means* | I've plenty of time; I've nothing special to do |

**Fill in the blanks with one of the idioms above so that each sentence makes sense.**

1. "I didn't go away for my vacation this year," Jane said when she returned to work. "And I wish I had gone some place. I got very bored because I had so much _____."

2. Mr. Brown asked his boss for a raise. "I'd like to give you more money," his boss said, "but business is so bad, _____."

3. "Hurry up! Hurry up! Let's go! We're going to be late," John yelled to his brother. "I'm coming as fast as I can," his brother answered, " _____ _____."

4. "Can you lend me $10? I've got a date tonight with Mary Anne, but I'm broke," Sam said to Ted. Ted just stared at him. "Are you kidding? You already owe me $20. _____."

5. "We had to fire her," the owner of the dress shop said. "She's a nice girl but she just _____."

Name _____ Date_____

# Which One Fits?

| | | |
|---|---|---|
| **You're pulling my leg** | *means* | You're joking |
| **Step on it!** | *means* | Hurry! |
| **Hold your horses** | *means* | Wait a minute |
| **Too many irons in the fire** | *means* | Trying to do too many things at one time |
| **In a jam** | *means* | In trouble |

***Fill in the blanks with one of the idioms above so that each sentence makes sense.***

1. She starts a lot of projects but she never seems to have time to finish one. She has _____ .

2. "What would you say if I told you I had won a million dollars?" Ken asked his friend. "I'd say _____ ," Bob answered.

3. "We only have 45 minutes to catch our plane," Fred said, "so you had better _____ ."

4. The little girl stamped her foot. "I want to go right now," she screamed. Her sister looked at her calmly. "Until I finish my homework, you're just going to have to _____ ."

5. Richie was talking to his friend on the telephone. "My father found out I wrecked his car," he said. "I'm _____ ."

Name _____ Date_____

# Which One Fits?

| | | |
|---|---|---|
| **Let your hair down** | *means* | Relax and share your thoughts and problems |
| **Lost his marbles** | *means* | Acts as if he's crazy |
| **Eat your (my) words** | *means* | You said something and now you wish you hadn't said it |
| **Cool your (his) heels** | *means* | Wait |
| **Face the music** | *means* | Be brave; take what's coming |

***Fill in the blanks with one of the idioms above so that each sentence makes sense.***

1. "I've been called to the principal's office," Tim said. "It's probably because I skipped school last week. I might as well go now and _____ _____."

2. "I saw a guy on TV last night who thought he was Napoleon," Meg said. "He had really _____."

3. I'm so ashamed. I asked my aunt if she had put on weight. She said she had just *lost* 15 pounds. I wish I could _____ .

4. Mr. Jones was angry. His doctor's appointment was for 4:00, and he had to _____ until almost 5:30.

5. "You keep all of your troubles bottled up inside," Karen said to Jan. "You need to _____."

Name _____ Date_____

# Create Your Own Colorful Sentences

*Select any 5 of the idioms below and write a sentence for each one that you choose.*

Keep your shirt on          Go fly a kite

Time on my hands          Can't cut the mustard

My hands are tied          Step on it

You're pulling my leg          Hold your horses

1. _____
   _____

2. _____
   _____

3. _____
   _____

4. _____
   _____

5. _____
   _____

*Can you think of any idioms? See if you can write 3 idioms below.*

1. _____

2. _____

3. _____

Name _____ Date_____

# Create Your Own Colorful Sentences

*Select any 5 of the idioms below and write a sentence for each one that you choose.*

Let your hair down          Lost his marbles

Eat your words              Cool your heels

Face the music              In a jam

Too many irons in the fire

1. _____
   _____

2. _____
   _____

3. _____
   _____

4. _____
   _____

5. _____
   _____

*Can you think of any idioms? See if you can write 3 idioms below.*

1. _____

2. _____

3. _____

Name _____ Date_____

# Verbs and Nouns

## *Verbs*

A.  Not all of the idioms you have been studying in Lesson 1 have verbs in them. But most do. Study the idioms listed on page 5. Can you find 2 verbs that begin with the letter **f**?

  _____          _____

B.  How about 2 verbs that begin with the letter **c**?

  _____          _____

C.  Do you see 2 verbs that begin with the letter **l**?

  _____          _____

## *Nouns*

D.  There are 4 nouns in the list of idioms on page 5 that refer to things that are a part of you. List them here.

  _____          _____

  _____          _____

E.  Two nouns refer to something that you can eat.

  _____          _____

F.  Two nouns refer to something children use when they want to have fun.

  _____          _____

G.  List 3 more nouns in the list of idioms.

  _____          _____

Name _____ Date_____

# Unscramble the Words

*First, unscramble the words below, then list them in alphabetical order. (All of these words come from the idioms listed on page 5.)*

1.  D T A M R S U      M __ __ __ __ __ __

2.  S H O S E R      H __ __ __ __ __

3.  E L M R A S B      M __ __ __ __ __ __

4.  L E E S H      H __ __ __ __

5.  N O I R S      I __ __ __ __

6.  L G P L U N I      P __ __ __ __ __ __

7.  R S T I H      S __ __ __ __

8.  I S C U M      M __ __ __ __

9.  O S D W R      W __ __ __ __

10. D N A S H      H __ __ __ __

1.  _____
2.  _____
3.  _____
4.  _____
5.  _____
6.  _____
7.  _____
8.  _____
9.  _____
10. _____

## Activity 1

**A**

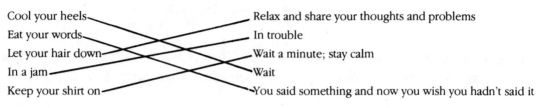

Cool your heels — Wait a minute; stay calm
Eat your words — In trouble
Let your hair down — Relax and share your thoughts and problems
In a jam — You said something and now you wish you hadn't said it
Keep your shirt on — Wait

**B**

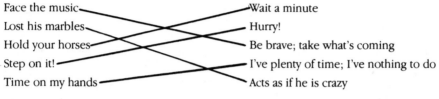

Face the music — Be brave; take what's coming
Lost his marbles — Acts as if he is crazy
Hold your horses — Wait a minute
Step on it! — Hurry!
Time on my hands — I've plenty of time; I've nothing to do

**C**

Go fly a kite — Get away from me; leave me alone
Can't cut the mustard — Can't measure up to expectations; can't do it
My hands are tied — I can't do anything about it
You're pulling my leg — You're joking
Too many irons in the fire — Trying to do too many things at one time

## Activity 2

1. Time on my hands
2. My hands are tied
3. Keep your shirt on
4. Go fly a kite
5. Can't cut the mustard

## Activity 3

1. Too many irons in the fire
2. You're pulling my leg
3. Step on it
4. Hold your horses
5. In a jam

## Activity 4

1. Face the music
2. Lost his marbles
3. Eat my words
4. Cool his heels
5. Let your hair down

## Activity 7

A. fly, face
B. cut, cool
C. let, lost
D. hands, leg, hair, heels
E. mustard, jam
F. kite, marbles
G. shirt, horses, irons, fire, words, music

## Activity 8

1. mustard
2. horses
3. marbles
4. heels
5. irons
6. pulling
7. shirt
8. music
9. words
10. hands

1. hands
2. heels
3. horses
4. irons
5. marbles
6. music
7. mustard
8. pulling
9. shirt
10. words

## What Idioms Mean

I'm in the doghouse.

| | | |
|---|---|---|
| **In the dark** | *means* | Don't understand or are ignorant about something |
| **A dime a dozen** | *means* | Very cheap; available; easy to find |
| **You're in the doghouse** | *means* | Someone is very angry at you |
| **Bury the hatchet** | *means* | Forgive and forget |
| **Call it a day** | *means* | Stop whatever you are doing |
| **Put your cards on the table** | *means* | Be honest; share all the facts |
| **It's raining cats and dogs** | *means* | It's raining very hard |
| **A chip on your shoulder** | *means* | Looking for an excuse to fight |
| **Barking up the wrong tree** | *means* | Making an error in judgment or action |
| **Beat around the bush** | *means* | Not coming to the point of a subject |
| **Bend an ear** | *means* | Listen; pay attention |
| **Don't breathe a word** | *means* | Keep a secret |
| **Down in the mouth** | *means* | Very sad |
| **Draw a blank** | *means* | Can't remember |
| **On top of the world** | *means* | Feeling great |

Name _____ Date_____

# Matching

*Draw a line to connect the idiom to its correct meaning. The first one has been done for you.*

### A

In the dark                          Very cheap

On top of the world                  Someone is very angry at you

A dime a dozen                       Can't remember

Draw a blank                         Don't understand or are ignorant about
                                     something

You're in the doghouse               Feeling great

### B

Bury the hatchet                     Stop whatever you are doing

Down in the mouth                    Forgive and forget

Call it a day                        Keep a secret

Don't breathe a word                 Be honest; share all the facts

Put your cards on the table          Very sad

### C

It's raining cats and dogs           Looking for an excuse to fight

Bend an ear                          Not coming to the point of a subject

A chip on your shoulder              Making an error in judgment or action

Beat around the bush                 Listen; pay attention

Barking up the wrong tree            It's raining very hard

Name _____ Date_____

# Which One Fits?

| | | |
|---|---|---|
| **In the dark** | *means* | Don't understand or are ignorant about something |
| **You're in the doghouse** | *means* | Someone is very angry at you |
| **A dime a dozen** | *means* | Very cheap; available; easy to find |
| **Bury the hatchet** | *means* | Forgive and forget |
| **Call it a day** | *means* | Stop whatever you are doing |

*Fill in the blanks with one of the idioms above so that each sentence makes sense.*

1. Good friends Bob and George had been angry at each other for a week. Finally Bob went to see George and said, "This fight has been going on too long. Let's _____ ."

2. At five o'clock Mary put the cover on her typewriter, leaned back in her chair, and said, "I'm tired. I think I'll _____ and go home."

3. Allen was telling his father about jobhunting. "Good jobs are hard to find. But jobs that don't pay much and have long hours are _____ _____ ."

4. "Your brother has been looking all over for you," Tom said. "He told me you were supposed to be back home at five o'clock and now it's almost seven. I think _____ ."

5. "Don't tell her about our little secret," whispered Mary. "Let's just keep her _____ ."

Name _____ Date_____

# Which One Fits?

Put your cards on the table     *means*     Be honest; share all the facts

It's raining cats and dogs     *means*     It's raining very hard

A chip on your (his) shoulder     *means*     Looking for an excuse to fight

Barking up the wrong tree     *means*     Making an error in judgment or action

Beat around the bush     *means*     Not coming to the point of a subject

*Fill in the blanks with one of the idioms above so that each sentence makes sense.*

1.  "Before we can make a deal," Mr. Jones said, "you are going to have to be honest with me and _____."

2.  "I don't know what's wrong with Bill," his coach said. "He seems upset and angry. Every day when he comes to practice he has _____ _____."

3.  I can't stand Jack. He never gives the facts. All he does is _____ _____ .

4.  "I was going to go for a walk earlier today," Joanne said, "but the weather is awful. _____."

5.  I thought Jill liked me a lot. But today I saw her taking a walk with Ted. I was really _____ .

Name _____ Date_____

# Which One Fits?

| | | |
|---|---|---|
| **Bend an ear** | *means* | Listen; pay attention |
| **Don't breathe a word** | *means* | Keep a secret |
| **Down in the mouth** | *means* | Very sad |
| **Draw a blank** | *means* | Can't remember |
| **On top of the world** | *means* | Feeling great |

*Fill in the blanks with one of the idioms above so that each sentence makes sense.*

1. "We want Betty's party to be a surprise," Ellen said, "so _____

   _____ to anyone about it."

2. Is something wrong? You have looked so _____

   _____ all day.

3. I try and try to remember people's names when I'm introduced to them

   but sometimes I just _____ .

4. "I have an important announcement," the teacher said, "so I want

   everyone in the class to _____ ."

5. Hooray! My dad said he is going to get me a car for a graduation present.

   I'm _____ .

Name _____ Date_____

# Create Your Own Colorful Sentences

*Select any 5 of the idioms below and write a sentence for each one that you choose.*

| | |
|---|---|
| **In the dark** | **A dime a dozen** |
| **You're in the doghouse** | **Bury the hatchet** |
| **Call it a day** | **Put your cards on the table** |
| **It's raining cats and dogs** | **A chip on your shoulder** |

1. _____
   _____

2. _____
   _____

3. _____
   _____

4. _____
   _____

5. _____
   _____

*Can you think of any idioms? See if you can write 3 idioms below.*

1. _____

2. _____

3. _____

Name _____ Date_____

# Create Your Own Colorful Sentences

*Select any 5 of the idioms below and write a sentence for each one that you choose.*

Barking up the wrong tree          Beat around the bush

Bend an ear                        Don't breathe a word

Down in the mouth                  Draw a blank

On top of the world

1. _____
   _____

2. _____
   _____

3. _____
   _____

4. _____
   _____

5. _____
   _____

*Can you think of any idioms? See if you can write 3 idioms below.*

1. _____

2. _____

3. _____

Name _____ Date_____

# Verbs and Nouns

## *Verbs*

A.  Not all of the idioms you have been studying in Lesson 2 have verbs in them. But most do. Study the idioms listed on page 15. There are 5 verbs that begin with the letter **b**. Find at least four of them.

_____        _____

_____        _____

B.  Write down one verb that begins with the letter **d**.

_____

C.  Can you find one verb that begins with the letter **p**?

_____

## *Nouns*

D.  There are 3 nouns you might find in your back yard.

_____      _____      _____

E.  Two nouns name things you will find on your head.

_____        _____

F.  There are two nouns that begin with the letters **w-o-r**.

_____        _____

G.  List 3 more nouns in the list of idioms.

_____      _____      _____

Name _____ Date_____

# Unscramble the Words

*First, unscramble the words below, then list them in alphabetical order.*
*(All of these words come from the idioms listed on page 15.)*

1. Z N O D E          D __ __ __ · __

2. S H O G U D E O      D __ __ __ __ __ __ __

3. T U H O M         M __ __ __ __

4. T H E C H T A       H __ __ __ __ __ __

5. G N A N I I R       R __ __ __ __ __ __

6. L B K N A         B __ __ __ __

7. L U O H E R S D      S __ __ __ __ __ __ __

8. G R A B N I K       B __ __ __ __ __ __

9. D W R O L         W __ __ __ __

10. E T A B E R H       B __ __ __ __ __ __

1. _____

2. _____

3. _____

4. _____

5. _____

6. _____

7. _____

8. _____

9. _____

10. _____

## *Activity 1*

**A**

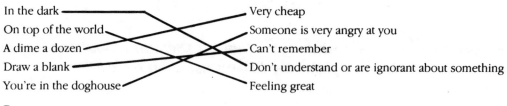

In the dark — Very cheap
On top of the world — Someone is very angry at you
A dime a dozen — Can't remember
Draw a blank — Don't understand or are ignorant about something
You're in the doghouse — Feeling great

**B**

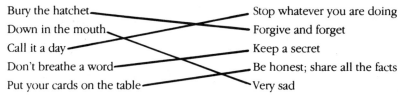

Bury the hatchet — Stop whatever you are doing
Down in the mouth — Forgive and forget
Call it a day — Keep a secret
Don't breathe a word — Be honest; share all the facts
Put your cards on the table — Very sad

**C**

It's raining cats and dogs — Looking for an excuse to fight
Bend an ear — Not coming to the point of a subject
A chip on your shoulder — Making an error in judgment or action
Beat around the bush — Listen; pay attention
Barking up the wrong tree — It's raining very hard

## *Activity 2*

1. Bury the hatchet
2. Call it a day
3. A dime a dozen
4. You're in the doghouse
5. In the dark

## *Activity 3*

1. Put your cards on the table
2. A chip on his shoulder
3. Beat around the bush
4. It's raining cats and dogs
5. Barking up the wrong tree

## *Activity 4*

1. Don't breathe a word
2. Down in the mouth
3. Draw a blank
4. Bend an ear
5. On top of the world

## *Activity 7*

A. bury, barking, beat, bend, breathe
B. draw
C. put
D. doghouse, tree, bush
E. ear, mouth
F. word, world

## *Activity 8*

1. dozen
2. doghouse
3. mouth
4. hatchet
5. raining
6. blank
7. shoulder
8. barking
9. world
10. breathe

1. barking
2. blank
3. breathe
4. doghouse
5. dozen
6. hatchet
7. mouth
8. raining
9. shoulder
10. world

## What Idioms Mean

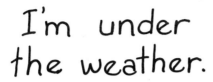 

I'm under the weather.

| | | |
|---|---|---|
| **Wave the white flag** | *means* | Surrender; give up |
| **Under the weather** | *means* | Sick; not feeling well |
| **Wet your whistle** | *means* | Have a drink |
| **Out of whack** | *means* | Broken; not working |
| **Wipe the slate clean** | *means* | Start over; a fresh beginning |
| **Keep on your toes** | *means* | Stay alert |
| **She twisted my arm** | *means* | She persuaded me (almost against my better judgment) |
| **Don't spill the beans** | *means* | Don't tell anyone; keep a secret |
| **Fit to be tied** | *means* | Very angry or upset |
| **It took the wind out of my sails** | *means* | It shocked or disappointed me |
| **Take a load off** | *means* | Sit down and relax |
| **He throws his weight around** | *means* | He brags a lot and tries to act important |
| **Time flies** | *means* | Time passes quickly |
| **Pull yourself together** | *means* | Calm down |
| **We were in stitches** | *means* | We were laughing very hard |

Name _____ Date_____

# Matching

*Draw a line to connect the idiom to its correct meaning. The first one has been done for you.*

## A

Wave the white flag                            Have a drink

Under the weather                          Broken; not working

Wet your whistle                          Start over; a fresh beginning

Out of whack                          Surrender; give up

Wipe the slate clean                          Sick; not feeling well

## B

Keep on your toes                          Don't tell anyone; keep a secret

She twisted my arm                          Stay alert

Don't spill the beans                          Very angry or upset

Fit to be tied                          It shocked or disappointed me

It took the wind out of my sails              She persuaded me (almost against my better judgment)

## C

Take a load off                          We were laughing very hard

He throws his weight around              Calm down

Time flies                          Sit down and relax

Pull yourself together                      Time passes quickly

We were in stitches                        He brags a lot and tries to act important

Name _____ Date _____

# Which One Fits?

| | | |
|---|---|---|
| **Wave the white flag** | *means* | Surrender; give up |
| **Out of whack** | *means* | Broken; not working |
| **She twisted my arm** | *means* | She persuaded me (almost against my better judgment) |
| **Take a load off** | *means* | Sit down and relax |
| **We were in stitches** | *means* | We were laughing very hard |

***Fill in the blanks with one of the idioms above so that each sentence makes sense.***

1.  The army had run out of food and water. There were many wounded men,

    so they decided to _____ .

2.  "You look tired. Come on in and _____ .

    I'll fix you a cold drink," Joan said to her friend.

3.  You must go and see that movie. It's one of the funniest we've seen in a

    long time. _____ from

    the beginning to the end.

4.  "I really wasn't in the mood to go to the beach with her today," Pam said,

    "but _____ , and I really

    had a pretty good time."

5.  "I'm going to have to call a repair man," Aunt Helen said. "The refrigerator

    is clearly _____ ."

Name _____ Date_____

# Which One Fits?

| | | |
|---|---|---|
| **Under the weather** | *means* | Sick; not feeling well |
| **Wipe the slate clean** | *means* | Start over; a fresh beginning |
| **Don't spill the beans** | *means* | Don't tell anyone; keep a secret |
| **He throws his weight around** | *means* | He brags a lot and tries to act important |
| **Pull yourself together** | *means* | Calm down |

*Fill in the blanks with one of the idioms above so that each sentence makes sense.*

1.  "It's all over now," Jim said to his brother. "You can stop shaking and

    crying and _____ ."

2.  I'm not going to school today. It's not because we are going to have a

    history exam. I'm really feeling _____ .

3.  "I always like to see January 1st roll around," Jason said. "It means I can

    _____ .

4.  Bob wonders why he's not invited to parties. No one wants to be around

    him because _____ so much.

5.  Mary and her sister were shopping. "I'm going to get Mom and Dad a

    toaster for Christmas this year," Mary said. "I want it to be a surprise so

    please _____ ."

Name _____ Date_____

# Which One Fits?

| | | |
|---|---|---|
| **Wet your whistle** | *means* | Have a drink |
| **Keep on your toes** | *means* | Stay alert |
| **Fit to be tied** | *means* | Very angry or upset |
| **It took the wind out of my sails** | *means* | It shocked or disappointed me |
| **Time flies** | *means* | Time passes quickly |

***Fill in the blanks with one of the idioms above so that each sentence makes sense.***

1.  "Hey, Joe, you've been chopping wood for an hour," Ron said. "You look
    hot. Come in the house and _____ ."

2.  "I can't believe it's midnight already," Matt said to Tim. "_____
    _____ when you're having fun."

3.  If you want to get high grades, be on the football team, and hold down a
    part-time job, you'll have to _____ .

4.  "When my folks found out that I didn't want to go to college," Susan said,
    "they were _____ .

5.  "When Ann said she didn't want to go to the dance with me _____
    _____ ," complained Terry.

Name _____ Date_____

# Create Your Own Colorful Sentences

*Select any 5 of the idioms below and write a sentence for each one that you choose.*

| | |
|---|---|
| Wave the white flag | Under the weather |
| Wet your whistle | Out of whack |
| Wipe the slate clean | Keep on your toes |
| She twisted my arm | Don't spill the beans |

1. _____

_____

2. _____

_____

3. _____

_____

4. _____

_____

5. _____

_____

*Can you think of any idioms? See if you can write 3 idioms below.*

1. _____

2. _____

3. _____

Name _____ Date_____

# Create Your Own Colorful Sentences

*Select any 5 of the idioms below and write a sentence for each one that you choose.*

Fit to be tied                    Take a load off

Time flies                        Pull yourself together

We were in stitches               He throws his weight around

It took the wind out of my sails

1. _____
   _____

2. _____
   _____

3. _____
   _____

4. _____
   _____

5. _____
   _____

*Can you think of any idioms? See if you can write 3 idioms below.*

1. _____

2. _____

3. _____

Name _____ Date_____

# Verbs and Adjectives

## Verbs

A.  Not all of the idioms you have been studying in Lesson 3 have verbs in them. But most do. Study the idioms listed on page 25. There are 5 verbs that begin with the letter **t**. Find at least 4 of them.

_____          _____

_____          _____

B.  Four verbs begin with **w**. Write down three of them.

_____   _____   _____

C.  Can you find 2 verbs that end in **ll** (double l)?

_____          _____

## Adjectives

The following are 12 nouns from the idioms on page 25. Choose any 8 nouns and write an adjective (a word that describes) before each noun that begins with the same letter as the noun. Two have been done for you.

1.  flag     *faded flag*
2.  weather     *warm weather*
3.  whistle     _____
4.  slate     _____
5.  toe     _____
6.  beans     _____
7.  wind     _____
8.  sails     _____
9.  load     _____
10. weight     _____
11. time     _____
12. stitches     _____

Name _____ Date_____

# Unscramble the Words

*First, unscramble the words below, then list them in alphabetical order.*
*(All of these words come from the idioms listed on page 25.)*

1.  H R T E E A W        W __ __ __ __ __ __

2.  T S I H L W E        W __ __ __ __ __ __

3.  D S E W I T T        T __ __ __ __ __ __

4.  I T E H W G          W __ __ __ __ __

5.  T E A S L            S __ __ __ __

6.  F S L R E U O Y      Y __ __ __ __ __ __ __

7.  H S C E T T I S      S __ __ __ __ __ __ __

8.  N E U R D            U __ __ __ __

9.  H R T E E O G T      T __ __ __ __ __ __ __

10. W H T S R O          T __ __ __ __ __

1. _____

2. _____

3. _____

4. _____

5. _____

6. _____

7. _____

8. _____

9. _____

10. _____

## Activity 1

**A**

Wave the white flag — Have a drink
Under the weather — Broken; not working
Wet your whistle — Start over; a fresh beginning
Out of whack — Surrender; give up
Wipe the slate clean — Sick; not feeling well

**B**

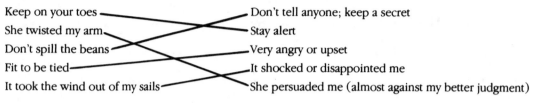

Keep on your toes — Don't tell anyone; keep a secret
She twisted my arm — Stay alert
Don't spill the beans — Very angry or upset
Fit to be tied — It shocked or disappointed me
It took the wind out of my sails — She persuaded me (almost against my better judgment)

**C**

Take a load off — We were laughing very hard
He throws his weight around — Calm down
Time flies — Sit down and relax
Pull yourself together — Time passes quickly
We were in stitches — He brags a lot and tries to act important

## Activity 2

1. Wave the white flag
2. Take a load off
3. We were in stitches
4. She twisted my arm
5. Out of whack

## Activity 3

1. Pull yourself together
2. Under the weather
3. Wipe the slate clean
4. He throws his weight around
5. Don't spill the beans

## Activity 4

1. Wet your whistle
2. Time flies
3. Keep on your toes
4. Fit to be tied
5. It took the wind out of my sails

## Activity 7

A. twisted, tied, took, take, throws
B. wave, wet, wipe, were
C. spill, pull

## Activity 8

| | |
|---|---|
| 1. weather | 1. slate |
| 2. whistle | 2. stitches |
| 3. twisted | 3. throws |
| 4. weight | 4. together |
| 5. slate | 5. twisted |
| 6. yourself | 6. under |
| 7. stitches | 7. weather |
| 8. under | 8. weight |
| 9. together | 9. whistle |
| 10. throws | 10. yourself |

34

## What Idioms Mean

I'm burning the candle at both ends.

| | | |
|---|---|---|
| Take a shot at it | *means* | Try it |
| That idea went up in smoke | *means* | That idea didn't work; disappeared; no one liked it |
| She was swept off her feet | *means* | She fell in love quickly |
| I was hot and bothered | *means* | I was upset |
| He kicked the bucket | *means* | He died |
| Pass the buck | *means* | Expect someone else to take the blame or responsibility |
| At the drop of a hat | *means* | Quickly; without advance notice |
| Down in the dumps | *means* | Depressed; gloomy; sad |
| Make both ends meet | *means* | Income = outgo |
| Break the ice | *means* | Prepare the way; start a conversation |
| It's all cut and dried | *means* | It's all settled |
| On the edge of tears | *means* | About to cry |
| Burn the candle at both ends | *means* | Too much work or play; not enough rest |
| He's too big for his britches | *means* | He thinks he's more important than he really is |
| On the double | *means* | Hurry! |

Name _____ Date_____

# Matching

*Draw a line to connect the idiom to its correct meaning. The first one has been done for you.*

**A**

Take a shot at it                    That idea didn't work; disappeared; no one liked it

That idea went up in smoke       He died

She was swept off her feet        She fell in love quickly

I was hot and bothered          Try it

He kicked the bucket           I was upset

**B**

Pass the buck                    Income = outgo

Down in the dumps          Expect someone else to take the blame or responsibility

Make both ends meet         Prepare the way; start a conversation

Break the ice                   It's all settled

It's all cut and dried          Depressed; gloomy; sad

**C**

At the drop of a hat          Too much work or play; not enough rest

Burn the candle at both ends     Hurry!

He's too big for his britches      Quickly; without advance notice

On the double                 About to cry

On the edge of tears         He thinks he's more important than he really is

Name _____ Date_____

# Which One Fits?

| | | |
|---|---|---|
| **Take a shot at it** | *means* | Try it |
| **That idea went up in smoke** | *means* | That idea didn't work; disappeared; no one liked it |
| **She was swept off her feet** | *means* | She fell in love quickly |
| **I was hot and bothered** | *means* | I was upset |
| **He kicked the bucket** | *means* | He died |

***Fill in the blanks with one of the idioms above so that each sentence makes sense.***

1. She knew him only two weeks before they were married. I suppose that

   _____ .

2. That poor old mule was deaf and almost blind and could hardly walk. It is

   probably just as well that _____ .

3. "I wanted to drop out of school and get a job," Cassie said, "but when my

   folks heard about it, _____ ."

4. You'll never know if you can do something until you try. Why don't you

   _____ .

5. "I thought I had done well on the history exam," Peter said. "When I

   found out I had failed it, _____ ."

Name _____ Date_____

# Which One Fits?

| | | |
|---|---|---|
| **Pass the buck** | *means* | Expect someone else to take the blame or responsibility |
| **At the drop of a hat** | *means* | Quickly; without advance notice |
| **Down in the dumps** | *means* | Depressed; gloomy; sad |
| **Break the ice** | *means* | Prepare the way; start a conversation |
| **Make both ends meet** | *means* | Income = outgo |

*Fill in the blanks with one of the idioms above so that each sentence makes sense.*

1. "Every month I work out a budget," groaned Ed. "I try to stick to it but somehow I can never _____ ."

2. It doesn't matter if she has homework or not, she's always ready to go to a party _____ .

3. "He makes me so mad," Kitty said. "The accident was all his fault but as usual I know he will try to _____ ."

4. When you are the new kid on the block trying to make friends, it is sometimes difficult to _____ .

5. "I tried my best to cheer him up," Ricky said, "but he has been _____ _____ all week."

Name _____ Date_____

# Which One Fits?

| | | |
|---|---|---|
| **On the edge of tears** | *means* | About to cry |
| **It's all cut and dried** | *means* | It's all settled |
| **Burn the candle at both ends** | *means* | Too much work or play; not enough rest |
| **He's too big for his britches** | *means* | He thinks he's more important than he really is |
| **On the double** | *means* | Hurry! |

**Fill in the blanks with one of the idioms above so that each sentence makes sense.**

1.  Ever since her dog died last week, she's been _____ _____ .

2.  "Students," called the coach, "I want you all to line up here _____ _____ ."

3.  "I don't want to go to camp but my parents say I've got to," Fred said. "I guess _____ ."

4.  You are going to get sick if you continue to _____ _____ .

5.  "I wish Brad weren't in my class," said Greg. "He brags all the time. Really, _____ ."

Name _____ Date_____

# Create Your Own Colorful Sentences

*Select any 5 of the idioms below and write a sentence for each one that you choose.*

| | |
|---|---|
| Take a shot at it | That idea went up in smoke |
| Pass the buck | She was swept off her feet |
| Break the ice | I was hot and bothered |
| Burn the candle at both ends | He kicked the bucket |

1. _____
   _____

2. _____
   _____

3. _____
   _____

4. _____
   _____

5. _____
   _____

*Can you think of any idioms? See if you can write 3 idioms below.*

1. _____

2. _____

3. _____

Name _____ Date_____

# Create Your Own Colorful Sentences

*Select any 5 of the idioms below and write a sentence for each one that you choose.*

Down in the dumps                 At the drop of a hat

Make both ends meet                It's all cut and dried

On the double                     On the edge of tears

He's too big for his britches

1. _____
   _____

2. _____
   _____

3. _____
   _____

4. _____
   _____

5. _____
   _____

*Can you think of any idioms? See if you can write 3 idioms below.*

1. _____

2. _____

3. _____

Name _____ Date_____

# Prepositions and Adjectives

## *Prepositions*

A.  The preposition **at** appears in 3 idioms on page 35. Write 3 short sentences using the preposition **at**.

    1. _____

    2. _____

    3. _____

B.  The preposition **of** appears in 2 idioms. Write 2 short sentences using the preposition **of**.

    1. _____

    2. _____

C.  The preposition **for** appears in 1 idiom. Write 1 short sentence using the preposition **for**.

    1. _____

## *Adjectives*

The following are 12 nouns from the idioms on page 35. Choose any 8 nouns and write an adjective (a word that describes) before each noun that begins with the same letter as the noun. Two have been done for you.

  1.  feet      *flat feet*

  2.  bucket    *brown bucket*

  3.  smoke    _____

  4.  hat       _____

  5.  tears     _____

  6.  ice       _____

  7.  candle    _____

  8.  britches   _____

  9.  shot      _____

10.  drop      _____

11.  edge      _____

12.  ends      _____

Name _____ Date _____

# Unscramble the Words

***First, unscramble the words below, then list them in alphabetical order. (All of these words come from the idioms listed on page 35.)***

1. K S E O M            S __ __ __ __
2. H E E B T O R D      B __ __ __ __ __ __ __
3. T K U E C B          B __ __ __ __ __
4. C K K E D I          K __ __ __ __ __
5. E C L A D N          C __ __ __ __ __
6. T E S H C R I B      B __ __ __ __ __ __ __
7. L E O U B D          D __ __ __ __ __
8. E I A D             I __ __ __
9. P S T W E            S __ __ __ __
10. K R A B E          B __ __ __ __

1. _____
2. _____
3. _____
4. _____
5. _____
6. _____
7. _____
8. _____
9. _____
10. _____

## Activity 1

**A**

Take a shot at it — That idea didn't work; disappeared; no one liked it

That idea went up in smoke — He died

She was swept off her feet — She fell in love quickly

I was hot and bothered — Try it

He kicked the bucket — I was upset

**B**

Pass the buck — Income = outgo

Down in the dumps — Expect someone else to take the blame or responsibility

Make both ends meet — Prepare the way; start a conversation

Break the ice — It's all settled

It's all cut and dried — Depressed; gloomy; sad

**C**

At the drop of a hat — Too much work or play; not enough rest

Burn the candle at both ends — Hurry!

He's too big for his britches — Quickly; without advance notice

On the double — About to cry

On the edge of tears — He thinks he's more important than he really is

## Activity 2

1. She was swept off her feet
2. He kicked the bucket
3. That idea went up in smoke
4. Take a shot at it
5. I was hot and bothered

## Activity 3

1. Make both ends meet
2. At the drop of a hat
3. Pass the buck
4. Break the ice
5. Down in the dumps

## Activity 4

1. On the edge of tears
2. On the double
3. It's all cut and dried
4. Burn the candle at both ends
5. He's too big for his britches

## Activity 8

| | |
|---|---|
| 1. smoke | 1. break |
| 2. bothered | 2. britches |
| 3. bucket | 3. bothered |
| 4. kicked | 4. bucket |
| 5. candle | 5. candle |
| 6. britches | 6. double |
| 7. double | 7. idea |
| 8. idea | 8. kicked |
| 9. swept | 9. smoke |
| 10. break | 10. swept |

# What Idioms Mean

It's on the tip of my tongue.

| | | |
|---|---|---|
| **Do you get my drift?** | *means* | Do you understand what I am saying? |
| **Put up a good front** | *means* | To act brave even if you don't feel that way |
| **That gets my goat** | *means* | That makes me angry |
| **I hope I make the grade** | *means* | I hope I succeed |
| **That goes against the grain** | *means* | That bothers or upsets me |
| **We're up a creek without a paddle** | *means* | We don't know what to do next; we've got a problem |
| **He's green around the gills** | *means* | He's feeling sick |
| **Other fish to fry** | *means* | Other things to do; other alternatives |
| **Through thick or thin** | *means* | Be there when things are good or bad |
| **Keep your shirt on** | *means* | Calm down |
| **On the tip of my tongue** | *means* | I know it but I can't quite say it |
| **She spoke with tongue in cheek** | *means* | She didn't really mean what she said; she was just kidding |
| **He pulled strings to get the job** | *means* | He got the job by using the influence of important people |
| **Drop in the bucket** | *means* | A small amount |
| **He has another card up his sleeve** | *means* | He's holding back another idea |

Name _____ Date_____

# Matching

*Draw a line to connect the idiom to its correct meaning. The first one has been done for you.*

## A

Do you get my drift?                    That makes me angry

Put up a good front                     I hope I succeed

That gets my goat                       That bothers or upsets me

I hope I make the grade                 Do you understand what I'm saying?

That goes against the grain             To act brave even if you don't feel that way

## B

We're up a creek without a paddle       We don't know what to do next; we've got a problem

He's green around the gills             Be there when things are good or bad

Other fish to fry                       Calm down

Through thick or thin                   Other things to do; other alternatives

Keep your shirt on                      He's feeling sick

## C

On the tip of my tongue                 He got the job by using the influence of important people

She spoke with tongue in cheek          A small amount

He pulled strings to get the job        I know it but I can't quite say it

Drop in the bucket                      He's holding back another idea

He has another card up his sleeve       She didn't really mean what she said; she was just kidding

Name _____ Date_____

# Which One Fits?

| | | |
|---|---|---|
| **Do you get my drift?** | *means* | Do you understand what I am saying? |
| **She gets my goat** | *means* | She makes me angry |
| **Put up a good front** | *means* | To act brave even if you don't feel that way |
| **I hope I make the grade** | *means* | I hope I succeed |
| **We're up a creek without a paddle** | *means* | We don't know what to do next; we've got a problem |

*Fill in the blanks with one of the idioms above so that each sentence makes sense.*

1.  "I told you once, and I'll tell you again," his sister said. "You cannot use

    my car. Now _____ ?"

2.  He had to give a speech in class. He was nervous but didn't want it to

    show. He hoped he could _____ .

3.  "Even though my marks weren't very good in high school," Sue said, "I

    want to go to college. _____ ."

4.  "I've told her not to call after ten o'clock, but she does it anyway," Kathy

    said, "even though she knows _____ ."

5.  No one remembered to bring matches to light a campfire, so _____

    _____ .

Name _____ Date_____

# Which One Fits?

| | | |
|---|---|---|
| **That goes against the grain** | *means* | That bothers or upsets me |
| **He's green around the gills** | *means* | He's feeling sick |
| **Through thick or thin** | *means* | Be there when things are good or bad |
| **Other fish to fry** | *means* | Other things to do; other alternatives |
| **Keep your shirt on** | *means* | Calm down |

*Fill in the blanks with one of the idioms above so that each sentence makes sense.*

1. "He never waits for his turn," Angela said. "He just shoves his way up to the head of the line. _____ ."

2. You should see Joe. He ate five bowls of chili and drank four cans of soda. Now _____ .

3. "She acted like she was too busy to go with us," Tina said. "I guess she has _____ ."

4. They have been friends since first grade. It's nice to see people stick together _____ .

5. "What's done is done," said Paul. "There's no point in getting upset about it so just _____ ."

Name _____ Date_____

# Which One Fits?

| | | |
|---|---|---|
| **On the tip of my tongue** | *means* | I know it but I can't quite say it |
| **She spoke with tongue in cheek** | *means* | She didn't really mean what she said; she was just kidding |
| **He pulled strings to get the job** | *means* | He got the job by using the influence of important people |
| **Drop in the bucket** | *means* | A small amount |
| **He has another card up his sleeve** | *means* | He's holding back another idea |

*Fill in the blanks with one of the idioms above so that each sentence makes sense.*

1. He didn't seem to mind when his boss turned down his first suggestion. I think it was because _____ .

2. "It drives me crazy," said Joan. "I've tried and tried to think of her last name, but I can't seem to remember it even though it's right _____ _____ ."

3. You may have saved up $200 for the club's plane fare for Europe but that is only a _____ .

4. "I heard her tell you she didn't care if she got asked to the prom but I think _____ ," Sue said.

5. Tom's grandfather owns the bank where Tim works as head cashier. I'm sure _____ .

Name _____ Date _____

# Create Your Own Colorful Sentences

*Select any 5 of the idioms below and write a sentence for each one that you choose.*

Do you get my drift?                Put up a good front

That gets my goat                   I hope I make the grade

That goes against the grain         We're up a creek without a paddle

He's green around the gills         Other fish to fry

1. _____

   _____

2. _____

   _____

3. _____

   _____

4. _____

   _____

5. _____

   _____

*Can you think of any idioms? See if you can write 3 idioms below.*

1. _____

2. _____

3. _____

Name _____ Date_____

# Create Your Own Colorful Sentences

*Select any 5 of the idioms below and write a sentence for each one that you choose.*

Through thick or thin                   Keep your shirt on

On the tip of my tongue                 She spoke with tongue in cheek

He pulled strings to get the job        Drop in the bucket

He has another card up his sleeve

1. _____
   _____

2. _____
   _____

3. _____
   _____

4. _____
   _____

5. _____
   _____

*Can you think of any idioms? See if you can write 3 idioms below.*

1. _____

2. _____

3. _____

Name _____ Date_____

# Beginning and Ending Sounds

## Beginning Sounds

A. Of the idioms listed on page 45, one idiom has 3 words that begin with the letters **th**. Use each of these words in a sentence.

   1. _____

   2. _____

   3. _____

B. Find two words that begin with a vowel. Use each of them in a sentence.

   1. _____

   2. _____

C. Quite a few words in the list of idioms on page 45 begin with the letter **g**. Choose any 2 and write 1 sentence that includes *both* words.

   1. _____

## Ending Sounds

D. Two words in the Lesson 5 idioms end in the letters **eek**. Write a sentence for each of these words.

   1. _____

   2. _____

E. Find a word that ends in 2 vowels. Use it in a sentence.

   1. _____

F. How many short words can you make out of the 6-letter word **bucket**? See if you can make at least 5.

   _____   _____   _____   _____   _____

Name _____ Date_____

# Unscramble the Words

### *First, unscramble the words below, then list them in alphabetical order. (All of these words come from the idioms listed on page 45.)*

1.  G E N O T U          T __ __ __ __ __
2.  R T F I D            D __ __ __ __
3.  C K E R E            C __ __ __ __
4.  T I S S G R N        S __ __ __ __ __ __
5.  K E B T U C          B __ __ __ __
6.  H A T E R O N        A __ __ __ __ __ __
7.  S I F H              F __ __ __
8.  H H O T U G R        T __ __ __ __ __ __
9.  V E E E S L          S __ __ __ __ __
10. S L I G L            G __ __ __ __

1.  _____
2.  _____
3.  _____
4.  _____
5.  _____
6.  _____
7.  _____
8.  _____
9.  _____
10. _____

## Activity 1

**A**

Do you get my drift? → Do you understand what I am saying?
Put up a good front → To act brave even if you don't feel that way
That gets my goat → That makes me angry
I hope I make the grade → I hope I succeed
That goes against the grain → That bothers or upsets me

**B**

We're up a creek without a paddle → We don't know what to do next; we've got a problem
He's green around the gills → He's feeling sick
Other fish to fry → Other things to do; other alternatives
Through thick or thin → Be there when things are good or bad
Keep your shirt on → Calm down

**C**

On the tip of my tongue → I know it but I can't quite say it
She spoke with tongue in cheek → She didn't really mean what she said; she was just kidding
He pulled strings to get the job → He got the job by using the influence of important people
Drop in the bucket → A small amount
He has another card up his sleeve → He's holding back another idea

## Activity 2

1. Do you get my drift?
2. Put up a good front
3. I hope I make the grade
4. She gets my goat
5. We're up a creek

## Activity 3

1. That goes against the grain
2. He's green around the gills
3. Other fish to fry
4. Through thick or thin
5. Keep your shirt on

## Activity 4

1. He has another card up his sleeve
2. On the tip of my tongue
3. Drop in the bucket
4. She spoke with tongue in cheek
5. He pulled strings to get the job

## Activity 7

A. Through thick or thin
B. against, around, another, up, in, etc.
C. get, grade, grain, gills, goat, good, etc.
D. creek, cheek
E. tongue
F. cub, cure, cube, cut, cue, but, buck, tuck, etc.

## Activity 8

1. tongue
2. drift
3. creek
4. strings
5. bucket
6. another
7. fish
8. through
9. sleeve
10. gills

1. another
2. bucket
3. creek
4. drift
5. fish
6. gills
7. sleeve
8. strings
9. through
10. tongue

## What Idioms Mean

My back is against the wall.

| | | |
|---|---|---|
| She keeps her nose to the grindstone | *means* | She gives all of her time and attention to her work |
| I hit the ceiling | *means* | I got very angry |
| Don't fly off the handle | *means* | Don't lose your temper |
| Don't bite off more than you can chew | *means* | Don't take on more projects than can comfortably handle |
| He's got ants in his pants | *means* | He's extremely nervous and excitable |
| Keep it under wraps | *means* | Don't tell anyone about it |
| Not give an inch | *means* | Take a position on a subject and not move from it |
| Keep a stiff upper lip | *means* | Be brave |
| I wash my hands of it | *means* | I give up; I won't have anything more to do with it |
| She's dragging her feet | *means* | She's going very slowly and delaying progress |
| Going around in circles | *means* | Confused; mixed up; don't know what to do next |
| Turn over a new leaf | *means* | Start or try again |
| Back is against the wall | *means* | Don't see any way out of a problem |
| Skating on thin ice | *means* | Doing something dangerous; asking for trouble |
| Get ahold of yourself | *means* | Calm down |

Name _____ Date _____

# Matching

*Draw a line to connect the idiom to its correct meaning. The first one has been done for you.*

## A

She keeps her nose to the grindstone    Don't lose your temper

I hit the ceiling    Don't take on more projects than you can comfortably handle

Don't fly off the handle    She gives all of her time and attention to her work

Don't bite off more than you can chew    He's extremely nervous and excitable

He's got ants in his pants    I got very angry

## B

Keep it under wraps    Be brave

Not give an inch    I give up; I won't have anything more to do with it

Keep a stiff upper lip    She's going very slowly and delaying progress

I wash my hands of it    Don't tell anyone about it

She's dragging her feet    Take a position on a subject and not move from it

## C

Going around in circles    Don't see any way out of a problem

Turn over a new leaf    Doing something dangerous; asking for trouble

Back is against the wall    Calm down

Skating on thin ice    Start or try again

Get ahold of yourself    Confused; mixed up; don't know what to do next

Name _____ Date_____

# Which One Fits?

| | | |
|---|---|---|
| **She keeps her nose to the grindstone** | *means* | She gives all of her time and attention to her work |
| **I hit the ceiling** | *means* | I got very angry |
| **Don't fly off the handle** | *means* | Don't lose your temper |
| **Don't bite off more than you can chew** | *means* | Don't take on more projects than you can comfortably handle |
| **He's got ants in his pants** | *means* | He's extremely nervous and excitable |

*Fill in the blanks with one of the idioms above so that each sentence makes sense.*

1. Betty's younger brother broke her stereo. "It was an accident," said her

   mother, "so _____ ."

2. He's so excited about the holidays, he can't sit still for two minutes. One

   would think _____ .

3. "She is one of our most valuable employees. _____

   _____ ," the president of the company said.

4. He goes to school, has a part-time job, plays football, and now he wants to

   join the drama club. I keep telling him, " _____

   _____ ."

5. When I found that someone had dented my car while it was in the parking

   lot, _____ .

Name _____ Date_____

# Which One Fits?

| | | |
|---|---|---|
| **Keep it under wraps** | *means* | Don't tell anyone about it |
| **Not give an inch** | *means* | Take a position on a subject and not move from it |
| **I wash my hands of it** | *means* | I give up; I won't have anything more to do with it |
| **Keep a stiff upper lip** | *means* | Be brave |
| **She's dragging her feet** | *means* | She's going very slowly and delaying progress |

*Fill in the blanks with one of the idioms above so that each sentence makes sense.*

1. I've tried my best to keep this club together, but no one will help me. So now _____ .

2. Johnny was disappointed because he couldn't go on the camping trips with his older brothers. "Don't cry," his mother said. "Perhaps you can go next year but now try to _____ ."

3. "We're trying to plan a surprise party for Lisa," Carol said. "Don't tell Mary. She's such a blabbermouth, she'll never be able to _____ _____ ."

4. He's the most stubborn man I know. I said I would meet him halfway but he will _____ .

5. Pam shows up late all the time when she knows there is work to be done. It is clear that _____ .

Name _____ Date_____

# Which One Fits?

| | | |
|---|---|---|
| **Going around in circles** | *means* | Confused; mixed up; don't know what to do next |
| **Back is against the wall** | *means* | Don't see any way out of a problem |
| **Turn over a new leaf** | *means* | Start again |
| **Skating on thin ice** | *means* | Doing something dangerous; asking for trouble |
| **Get ahold of yourself** | *means* | Calm down |

*Fill in the blanks with one of the idioms above so that each sentence makes sense.*

1. On January 1st I am going to _____ and stop smoking.

2. Fred was angry that the rain ruined his camping trip. He slammed the door and threw his gear on the floor. "That's enough," said his mother. "It's time for you to _____ ."

3. He has at least 10 tickets for speeding. Yet he still drives above the speed limit. I think he is _____ .

4. "Jill wants me to visit her on my vacation," said Marsha. "But Sue wants me to take a trip with her. I don't know what to do. I'm _____ _____ ."

5. "My car payment is due. I don't have the money, and I don't have a job," said Jake. "My _____ ."

Name _____ Date_____

# Create Your Own Colorful Sentences

*Select any 5 of the idioms below and write a sentence for each one that you choose.*

She keeps her nose to the grindstone        I hit the ceiling

Don't bite off more than you can chew        Don't fly off the handle

Keep it under wraps        Not give an inch

He's got ants in his pants        Keep a stiff upper lip

1. _____

   _____

2. _____

   _____

3. _____

   _____

4. _____

   _____

5. _____

   _____

*Can you think of any idioms? See if you can write 3 idioms below.*

1. _____

2. _____

3. _____

Name _____ Date_____

# Create Your Own Colorful Sentences

*Select any 5 of the idioms below and write a sentence for each one that you choose.*

I wash my hands of it                     She's dragging her feet

Going around in circles                   Turn over a new leaf

Back is against the wall                  Skating on thin ice

Get ahold of yourself

1. _____
   _____

2. _____
   _____

3. _____
   _____

4. _____
   _____

5. _____
   _____

*Can you think of any idioms? See if you can write 3 idioms below.*

1. _____

2. _____

3. _____

Name _____ Date_____

# Verbs and Nouns

## *Verbs*

A.  In the idioms listed on page 55 there are several verbs that have only 3 letters. Choose 3 of these and write a sentence for each one.

    1. _____

    2. _____

    3. _____

B.  There are 2 verbs that have to do with eating. Write a sentence for each one.

    1. _____

    2. _____

C.  Find 2 verbs that end in **ing** and write a sentence for each one.

    1. _____

    2. _____

## *Nouns*

D.  There are 4 nouns that name something on your head or body. Use all 4 of these in 2 sentences.

    1. _____

    2. _____

E.  There are 2 nouns that name a part of a room. Use each one in a sentence.

    1. _____

    2. _____

F.  Find 2 nouns that begin with the letter **i** and write them below.

    _____    _____

Name _____ Date_____

## Unscramble the Words

*First, unscramble the words below, then list them in alphabetical order.*
*(All of these words come from the idioms listed on page 55.)*

| | | |
|---|---|---|
| 1. | N I G I C L E | C __ __ __ __ __ __ |
| 2. | E D A L H N | H __ __ __ __ __ |
| 3. | P E P U R | U __ __ __ __ |
| 4. | S E C C L I R | C __ __ __ __ __ __ |
| 5. | S P R W A | W __ __ __ __ |
| 6. | F I S F T | S __ __ __ __ |
| 7. | U D O N A R | A __ __ __ __ __ |
| 8. | E P E S K | K __ __ __ __ |
| 9. | T A K N I S G | S __ __ __ __ __ __ |
| 10. | W E H C | C __ __ __ |

1. _____

2. _____

3. _____

4. _____

5. _____

6. _____

7. _____

8. _____

9. _____

10. _____

## Activity 1

**A**

She keeps her nose to the grindstone. ——— Don't lose your temper

I hit the ceiling ——— Don't take on more projects than you can comfortably handle

Don't fly off the handle ——— She gives all of her time and attention to her work

Don't bite off more than you can chew ——— He's extremely nervous and excitable

He's got ants in his pants ——— I got very angry

**B**

Keep it under wraps ——— Be brave

Not give an inch ——— I give up; I won't have anything more to do with it

Keep a stiff upper lip ——— She's going very slowly and delaying progress

I wash my hands of it ——— Don't tell anyone about it

She's dragging her feet ——— Take a position on a subject and not move from it

**C**

Going around in circles ——— Don't see any way out of a problem

Turn over a new leaf ——— Doing something dangerous; asking for trouble

Back is against the wall ——— Calm down

Skating on thin ice ——— Start or try again

Get ahold of yourself ——— Confused; mixed up; don't know what to do next

## Activity 2

1. Don't fly off the handle
2. He's got ants in his pants
3. She keeps her nose to the grindstone
4. Don't bite off more than you can chew
5. I hit the ceiling

## Activity 3

1. I wash my hands of it
2. Keep a stiff upper lip
3. Keep it under wraps
4. Not give an inch
5. She's dragging her feet

## Activity 4

1. Turn over a new leaf
2. Get ahold of yourself
3. Skating on thin ice
4. Going around in circles
5. Back is against the wall

## Activity 7

A. hit, fly, got, get
B. bite, chew
C. dragging, skating
D. nose, lip, hands, feet
E. ceiling, wall
F. inch, ice

## Activity 8

1. ceiling
2. handle
3. upper
4. circles
5. wraps
6. stiff
7. around
8. keeps
9. skating
10. chew

1. around
2. ceiling
3. chew
4. circles
5. handle
6. keeps
7. skating
8. stiff
9. upper
10. wraps